Printed in Italy.
Produced by Lloyd-Jones Ltd.
Designer: Mary pat Pino
Project editor: Jennifer Holder

ISBN: 0-7847-1432-0

09 08 07 06 05 04 03   9 8 7 6 5 4 3 2 1

GOD
THOUGHT OF IT
FIRST

written by
Joan N. Keener

illustrated by
Valeria Petrone

Standard
PUBLISHING
CINCINNATI, OHIO

God is the greatest inventor ever. It was God's idea to create the whole world and make everything in it, and he did!

People in God's world invent more amazing things that make our lives easier or better . . .

BUT GOD IS THE ONE WHO THOUGHT OF THEM FIRST!

A helicopter on a rescue mission flies up or down, backward or forward, and hovers in the air.

BUT GOD IS THE ONE WHO THOUGHT OF IT FIRST . . . .

HE MADE THE HUMMINGBIRD.

A hummingbird's wings beat fast and cause a humming sound. Hummingbirds can fly up or down, backward or forward, and they can hover in the air.

A submarine has special tanks that fill with water to make the sub sink. When the water is pumped out of the tanks, the sub rises.

BUT GOD IS THE ONE WHO THOUGHT OF IT FIRST . . .

HE MADE THE CHAMBERED NAUTILUS.

The bones of this sea creature form small "rooms," or chambers. The chambers empty or fill with water to make the little nautilus go up or down.

To walk over soft, deep snow without sinking, you wear snowshoes. And snow boots keep your feet warm.

But GOD IS THE ONE WHO THOUGHT OF IT FIRST . . . .

HE MADE THE SNOWSHOE RABBIT.

The rabbit's wide feet keep him on top of the snow. Long hairs grow on the sides of his feet and between his toes. The hairs help the rabbit's feet stay warm.

When you swim underwater, flippers can help your feet push the water so you can move forward.

BUT GOD IS THE ONE WHO THOUGHT OF IT FIRST . . .

HE MADE THE SEA LION. The sea lion's flippers push the water back so she can swim.

When you ride your bike or roller-skate, you wear a helmet and knee pads for protection.

BUT GOD IS THE ONE WHO THOUGHT OF IT FIRST . . .

HE MADE THE ARMADILLO. Hard plates protect this creature's body. The plates are jointed, so he can roll up in a ball for extra safety.

Photographers on safari wear camouflage so the animals won't see them and run away.

BUT GOD IS THE ONE WHO THOUGHT OF IT FIRST . . .

HE MADE THE CHAMELEON.

The chameleon's skin changes colors to match the surroundings so his enemies won't see him.

When you need to get clean, you take a shower. The water splashes all the dirt away.

BUT GOD IS THE ONE WHO THOUGHT OF IT FIRST . . .

HE MADE THE ELEPHANT.

The elephant uses his trunk like a shower. He squirts water all over his body to help him keep cool and clean.

A baby carrier lets parents keep their babies with
them wherever they go.

BUT GOD IS THE ONE WHO THOUGHT OF IT FIRST . . . .

HE MADE THE KANGAROO.

A mother kangaroo keeps her baby, called a "joey," in a pouch on the front of her body. She takes the little joey with her wherever she goes.

Suspended under long "wings" made of cloth, the pilot of a hang glider flies from place to place.

BUT GOD IS THE ONE WHO THOUGHT OF IT FIRST . . .

HE MADE THE FLYING SQUIRREL.

To glide from tree to tree, the flying squirrel spreads out the folds of skin between his front and back legs.

Night vision goggles use the light from the stars and moon to allow police officers to see better at night.

BUT GOD IS THE ONE WHO THOUGHT OF IT FIRST . . . .

Our world is full of things that began as good ideas,

BUT GOD IS THE ONE WHO THOUGHT OF THEM FIRST!